Qu
for Dinner

by Maryann Dobeck
illustrated by Joe Boddy

Scott Foresman

Editorial Offices: Glenview, Illinois • New York, New York
Sales Offices: Reading, Massachusetts • Duluth, Georgia
Glenview, Illinois • Carrollton, Texas • Menlo Park, California

"I want something new for dinner," says the King. "How about quail?"

"Fine," says the cook. And she
puts on her apron.

"Oh, no!" says Quail. "The King wants quail for dinner. I am in danger. I cannot stay here. I will have to run away by myself!"

On her way, Quail meets
Horse. He is pulling a cart.
"Where are you going?" asks Horse.

"Far, far away," says Quail.
"The King wants quail for dinner.
And the King always gets what
he wants."

On her way, Quail meets
Sheep. She is eating grass. "Why
are you rushing?" asks Sheep.

"The King wants quail for
dinner. And the King always
gets what he wants," says Quail.

On her way, Quail meets Pig.
He is rolling in mud. "What are
you doing?" asks Pig.

"I am going away," says Quail.
"The King wants quail for
dinner. And the King always
gets what he wants."

Pig says, "Just keep going. I
have a plan. We will find you later."
"Okay," says Quail.

Pig makes a sign. He puts it on the barn. It says:

Quail is a great mother.
She keeps her eggs warm.
She sits on them.
She sits until each one hatches.

Quail is a great mother.
She keeps her eggs warm.
She sits on them.
She sits until each one hatches.

The King and the cook are looking for Quail. As they pass the barn, they stop to read the new sign. Then the King asks, "Where is Quail?"

"I don't know," says Pig.

The sign reads:

Quail is a great mother. She watches her chicks. She keeps them safe.

Horse puts up a sign too.
It says:

Quail is a great mother.
She watches her chicks.
She keeps them safe.

On their way home, the King
and the cook read the new sign.
Then the King asks, "Have you
seen Quail?"

"She went away," says Horse.

Sheep gives the King a note.
It says:

I have gone away by myself.
I miss you and all my friends.

Quail

"Well, well," says the King.
"Quail misses me! Find her.
Then we will invite her to eat
dinner with us."

"What shall we eat?" asks
the cook.

"We can eat rice and beans,"
says the King.

"Rice and beans!" squeals Pig.

"Hooray!" snorts Horse.

"Hooray!" shouts Sheep.

"I will go find Quail," says Pig.

"I will go warm our dinner,"
says Cook.

"Hello, Quail," says the King.
"Join us for dinner. We will have
rice and beans. Bring all your
animal friends."

"Hooray!" yells Quail. "Hail to
the King!"

Phonics for Families: This book features words with the long *a* sound, such as *apron, quail*, and *way*, and words with endings *-ing, -s,* and *-es.* It also provides practice reading the words *mother, new, warm, keep,* and *myself.* Encourage your child to make a sign that uses some of these words.

Phonics Skills: Long *a* spelled *a, ai, ay*; Inflected endings *-es, -ing, -s* (without spelling change)

High-Frequency Words: *mother, new, warm, keep, myself*

Printed in the United States of America

ISBN 0-673-61202-3

3 4 5 6 7 8 9 10 - BISF - 06 05 04 03 02 01 00

Scott Foresman
Reading

Grade 2
Phonics Reader 6

Quail for Dinner
by Maryann Dobeck
illustrated by
Joe Boddy

Phonics Skills:
- Long *a* spelled *a, ai, ay*
- Inflected endings
  -es, -ing, -s (without
  spelling change)

Scott Foresman
Phonics System

Scott Foresman